Poetry Explorers

Scotland

Edited by Donna Samworth

First published in Great Britain in 2009 by

 Young**Writers**

Remus House
Coltsfoot Drive
Peterborough
PE2 9JX
Telephone: 01733 890066
Website: www.youngwriters.co.uk

Foreword

At Young Writers our defining aim is to promote an enjoyment of reading and writing amongst children and young adults. By giving aspiring poets the opportunity to see their work in print, their love of the written word as well as confidence in their own abilities has the chance to blossom.

Our latest competition Poetry Explorers was designed to introduce primary school children to the wonders of creative expression. They were given free reign to write on any theme and in any style, thus encouraging them to use and explore a variety of different poetic forms.

We are proud to present the resulting collection of regional anthologies which are an excellent showcase of young writing talent. With such a diverse range of entries received, the selection process was difficult yet very rewarding. From comical rhymes to poignant verses, there is plenty to entertain and inspire within these pages. We hope you agree that this collection bursting with imagination is one to treasure.

Contents

Taynuilt Primary School, Taynuilt

Torthorwald Primary School, Torthorwald

The Poems

Autumn

I see orange leaves on the ground
I hear leaves rustling in the wind
I smell bonfires burning dead leaves
I taste soft brambles at my house
I touch crunchy smooth leaves on the ground
I feel happy because Hallowe'en is in autumn.

Niamh Brady (7)
Arinagour Primary School, Isle of Coll

Autumn

I see red berries, green berries and blackberries
I see yellow leaves and nuts that fall and seeds that are falling
I hear the wind rustling in the trees and also grass under the trees
Leaves rustling in the trees and the people
Are picking autumn flowers that are under the trees
I taste red berries and blackberries
I touch squishy berries, apples, pears and prickly stems and thorns
I feel happy about autumn because it is Hallowe'en.

Hazel Smith (8)

Arinagour Primary School, Isle of Coll

Autumn

I see yellow leaves on the ground
I hear the wind howling in the kitchen and blowing the trees
I smell bonfires
I taste apples
I touch crunchy leaves on the autumn table
I am sad because it is cold and I can't go to sunny beaches.

Beth Jamieson (7)

Arinagour Primary School, Isle of Coll

Autumn

I see no green leaves
I see black brambles, orange and brown leaves
I hear the wind and I hear the leaves rustling in the trees
I hear bangs shooting from the guns
I smell yummy food like apples, pears and honey
I taste crunchy, juicy apples and pears
I touch crunchy bramble leaves and soft berries
I feel happy in autumn as I see all the nice colours
I feel sad when it's too windy
It's too strong and blows me away from my mummy.

Maria Macintyre (7)
Arinagour Primary School, Isle of Coll

Autumn

I see leaves burning red on the trees
I hear hedgehogs snoring in the whistling grass
I smell the wet bog over the hill
I taste brambles growing at my house
I touch thorns quickly
I feel happy because it will soon be winter
And I can build a snowman and make snowballs.

Aidan Mackay (6)
Arinagour Primary School, Isle of Coll

Autumn

I see berries
I see colourful berries, yellow, red, black, green
Purple, golden and brown
I hear nuts cracking and hedgehogs hibernating
I smell leaves under trees
I taste brambles, apples, pears and meat
I touch squishy brambles
I like autumn because it is Hallowe'en and Bonfire Night.

Alexandra May Young (8)
Arinagour Primary School, Isle of Coll

The Fishing Competition

I felt excited and happy
Boat engines roared as they motored out to sea
Sailing boats smoothly sailed into the bay
Josh came with me.

We walked onto the pier
I could smell the burgers from Nick's van
I cast my line out with feathers attached
A weight on the end of the line
I caught two little mackerel.

The fish were small and scaly
Wriggling about on the pier
I put them into a bag
They flipped and flapped around
I could hear other casts whirring.

We drove to the middle pier
Waited in the queue to weigh the fish
I came second in my age group and won £2
It was exciting, I was very happy.

Ross Cook (9)
Arinagour Primary School, Isle of Coll

Spotting A Kestrel

I spotted a kestrel on the way back from Maria's party
My dad thought it was a sparrowhawk
It was perching on the telephone cable
Which was swaying in the wind.

We drove past in the car, the bird flew from the cable
Hovering then swooping up and down, looking for prey
We stopped and watched for ages.

The wind was wailing, waves smacking the sand
It was getting dark
We drove off, I turned to watch the kestrel
It was still swooping up and down.

Alexander Wainwright (10)
Arinagour Primary School, Isle of Coll

The Picnic

Up near the loch we had a picnic
It was fun and I got wet
I could see the village
Seagulls circling above us
I felt excited.

Lambs were bleating
Dougie and Tasha talked about Pokémon
Mum and Dad unpacked the food
We were having fun.

I could smell peanut butter and jam sandwiches
Brambles and fish
I felt happy.

Cameron Wainwright (9)
Arinagour Primary School, Isle of Coll

The Wind And The Tent

Roaring wind woke me, I looked out
Half the tent collapsed and Dad was stuck
I woke my sister and squeezed through the gap in the door.

Dad woke up, held up the door and guided me through
Lexi watched from the other room
Together we were safe again.

We struggled to take down the tent
Folded it and put it into the boot of the car
We were about to drive away when,
'Stop!' someone shouted, 'come to our caravan for tea.'

We squeezed together in the caravan with the Wainwrights
Sheltering from the gusting wind
Ate muesli bars and drank juice
I felt comforted
Later I told Grandpa of our adventure.

Poppy Young (10)
Arinagour Primary School, Isle of Coll

The Stormy Night

Water everywhere
Waves crashing against rocks
Smell of smoke puffing out of chimneys
Rain was falling hard like hailstones
It was terrifying.

Large white yacht
Crashing against the middle pier
Everyone watching was panicking
I was too.

By morning most of the water had gone
Ditches were still overflowing
But it was a ferry day
Everyone in the village helped
I felt happy.

Ella Smalley (10)
Arinagour Primary School, Isle of Coll

Scotland

S cotland's a bonnie place. Wi' hills and mountains an'
C aves. There's nothin' like Scotland, it's my homeland an' I'm
   proud
O ch aye. There's nothin' like it. Wi' its forests an'
T rees, wi' lochs an' ponds, burns an' rivers. I
L ike so much the castles and towns, for it's my homeland
A n' I'm proud. There was never, nor ever will be, anythin' like
   Scotland's whiskys or its tartans or its belief in freedom
N ae, I'll need no sun. The snow buryin' the landscape, the
   suspicious mists an' fogs an' the rain as it faws tae doomsday,
   that's a' I need for sure
D are me to stay a year in Scotland's bonnie islands, an' I'll say yes
   an' go withoot lookin' back, for Scotland's my homeland an' I'm
   proud an' there's nowhere I'd like to be mair than me homeland
   och Scotland's a bonnie place.

Jonathan Coll Martin (11)
Auchlinloch Primary School, Auchlinloch

Snow

S now is falling everywhere, white, sparkling and bright
N ow it's time for fun to come, sledging, snowmen and snowball
   fights
O utside is the best place to be when snow is falling. Can't you see?
W inter weather - cold and inviting.

Kiran Talwar (10)

Auchlinloch Primary School, Auchlinloch

Spain

Spain's sunny
It's so hot
There's hotels nearly everywhere
The beach is blazing hot
There are more hotels than volcanoes
The Canary Islands are part of Spain
Spain is a very hot place
You have lots of fun
People live in Spain
Spain is glorious
Nice beaches
Spain.

Ross McCafferty (10)
Auchlinloch Primary School, Auchinloch

The Weather

S lowly falling from the sky, lying on the ground
N eatly making a soft blanket
O h wow, it is so soft
W heeee! The snow is perfect for sledging
F lying in the air like tiny stars
L ochs frozen, people ice skating
A trocious blizzards
K eeping warm by the cosy fire, drinking hot cocoa
E nding the winter is not as much fun
   but before it goes away . . . snowball fight!

Rhiannon Smith (9)
Auchlinloch Primary School, Auchinloch

Snow

S now is white, covering the ground like a glittering blanket

N ow we can go sledding and hear the snow crunching under
our boots

O h how I love building snowmen with a hat, scarf, two twigs and a
carrot nose

W hat fun we have in winter with all the snow.

Heidi Shona Campbell (10)

Auchlinloch Primary School, Auchinloch

Winter

W is for winter
I is for ice frozen on the pond
N is for nice cold day
T is for trees covered in snow
E is for everyone playing outside
R is for rivers that turn to ice.

Craig Grace (10)
Auchlinloch Primary School, Auchinloch

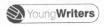

The War

The war
The war, I'd love to be in the war
It looks so much like fun
Having a gun and charging into war
Shooting, shooting everyone I see
Running madly with a gun
How I dream of being in the war
Hiding in bushes, shooting enemies that come by
How I dream of it every night
I guess it won't come true just now
I am still too small.

Calvin Chan (10)

Auchlinloch Primary School, Auchinloch

Anger

Anger is red like Hell
It tastes like drugs mixed with juice
It smells like the smoke of ashes
It looks like yellow bumps
It sounds like a baby shouting
Anger feels like thunder.

David McMillan (8)

Bargeddie Primary School, Bargeddie

Sadness

Sadness is like black clouds in the sky
It tastes like rotten apples
It smells like a hospital ward
It looks like kids fumbling in the dark
It sounds like a baby screaming and weeping
Sadness feels like a cold blanket reaching towards me.

Jillian O'Donnell (9)
Bargeddie Primary School, Bargeddie

Rainforest

R ainforest in the sun, if you gather it will be fun
A t the top, sit colourful birds
I nsects creeping, there are so many
N obody knows how many there are
F eeding, feeding on the leaves
O n the leaves sit frogs and spiders
R ushing rivers at the bottom
E ating, crunching monkeys on the trees
S ave the rainforest
T ry and save our world!

Callum Davies (10)
Bargeddie Primary School, Bargeddie

Scotland

S ghts are lovely, wonderful views
C aledonian dreams all around
O h such a faithful country
T in armour clanking in the castle
L adies sewing clothes together
A lovely place to live
N ow is the time to come and see such a wonderful place to be
D on't delay, come and see the loch at sunset dazzle.

Callum MacKinnon (9)
Bargeddie Primary School, Bargeddie

Spitefulness

S pitefulness is not for me
P ulling hair, I don't see
I don't see the fun in being mean
T ears of children, they should not be seen
E vil, horrible spitefulness, don't let it in
F ull of hatred, I don't want to be that way
U ncaring people will find out about you
L et them try to make me one
N o, I will not be one
E nd it all now
S pitefulness is not the way to be
S pitefulness should not live within me.

Emma Reid (8)
Bargeddie Primary School, Bargeddie

Rainforest

R ustling leaves on the ground
A mazon flowing through the forest
I s there an animal to be seen?
N ectar in the flowers, deep
F orest trees are so, so big
O n the floor the insects crawl
R ansacking and cutting down the forest
E mergent trees big and tall
S un beats down and rain drip-drops
T ry to save this world!

Thomas Smart (9)
Bargeddie Primary School, Bargeddie

Rainforest

R unning creatures everywhere
A mazing sights all about
I nsects crawling on the ground
N aughty animals creeping up behind you
F rogs jumping onto leaves
O xygen flowing in the air
R ivers passing smoothly
E very day you can hear the trees move
S ave the rainforest
T ry and save our world.

Ellie Devine (9)

Bargeddie Primary School, Bargeddie

Rabbie Burns

R abbie Burns the poet for Scotland
O ne poem he wrote was 'Auld Lang Syne'
B urns is loved by the whole world
E verybody knows he's famous
R abbie, a farmer's son
T elling stories in his poems

B urns suppers, they all love
U se his poems to celebrate Burns Night
R abbie Burns, his heart's in the Highlands
N ever wandered far from home
S cotland was his one true love.

Holly Hunter (9)
Bargeddie Primary School, Bargeddie

Spitefulness

S pitefulness is hurtful, cruel, it is not for me at all
P lease do not talk about me behind my back
I t is very hurtful when you hear it
T ears bring sadness
E very drop is horrible
F eeling awful, that's not for me
U gly tears bring red eyes
L unch alone, not for me
N o, no, come on, no crying
E ast to west, names are called
S adness came before happiness and it comes every day
S adness does not mix with love and happiness.

Emma Craig (8)
Bargeddie Primary School, Bargeddie

Rainforest

R iver Amazon flowing through the forest's floor
A nimals and birds catching food
I nsects crawling on the forest floor
N oises all around the rainforest
F orest floor has insects all around
O rang-utan red and so scary
R ound and about the animals
E ating, crunching on the trees
S ave the rainforest
T ry and save our world!

Danielle Adams (9)
Bargeddie Primary School, Bargeddie

Love

Love is pink and soft like a marshmallow
It tastes like a sweet cherry
It smells like gorgeous pouring chocolate
It looks like a big grin on my mum's face
It sounds like a sweet mellow tune
Love feels like the soft fur of a kitten.

Amy Sloan (7)
Bargeddie Primary School, Bargeddie

Seashore

S limy seaweed tickling my feet
E nchanting noisy mermaids creep
A ll around children playing
S un shines in the big blue sky
H eating up the pool for me
O ctopus playing with his friends, hoping his fun will never end
R ound about seashells sparkling
E els hand-in-hand, playing in the sand.

Jodie Govan (9)
Bargeddie Primary School, Bargeddie

Anger

Anger is red like burning lava
It tastes like juice mixed with drugs
It smells like smoky coal
It looks like it is the end of the world
It sounds like a storm
Anger feels like a burn from an iron.

Mitchell Loughlin (8)
Bargeddie Primary School, Bargeddie

Rainforest

R ustling trees and falling leaves
A nimals and birds catching food
I nsects fly over my head
N ever cut down the trees in the forest
F orests are in danger
O xygen is made in the forest
R ain and rivers flowing around the forest
E veryone loves the rainforest's fruits
S ave the rainforest
T ry and save the world!

Cerys Watson (8)
Bargeddie Primary School, Bargeddie

Rainforest

R ocks and rivers on the forest floor
A nimals and insects creeping around
I nsects making creepy noises
N uts and fruits falling off the trees
F alling leaves off the trees
O ver my head is the canopy
R ivers flowing through the forest floor
E xtraordinary
S ave the rainforest
T ry and save our world!

Emma McFarlane (8)
Bargeddie Primary School, Bargeddie

Happiness

Happiness is orange like the sunshine
It tastes like soft chocolate
It smells like fresh air
It looks like my mum's smiling face
It sounds like a melody
Happiness feels like water lapping on the beach.

Micayla Smith (9)

Bargeddie Primary School, Bargeddie

Seashore

S eaweed lying on the sand
E nchanting view as the water laps
A s all the children play all around
   and leave their footprints on the ground
S hells scattered in a mound
H ow you can hear all the waves
O ver, above, the sun shines
R eally excited, everyone plays
E veryone leaves with a happy face!

Gemma Woods (9)
Bargeddie Primary School, Bargeddie

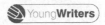

Space

Through the air, so far away
That's where the astronauts play
Peaceful, only stars, it's dark
Only you with a dream, no one left to nark
For that's where the dreams go, high in space
With only Saturn and Mars to chase.

Emma Patrick (11)

Christie Park Primary School, Alexandria

A Mysterious Journey

I cautiously step inside
My body trembling with fear
I look around the enclosed space
There is nobody here.

I pull the huge lever
Wondering what it will do
All of a sudden it starts to move
I wonder where it will take me to.

Suddenly it stops
I slowly open the door
I look around this strange place
I'm not in 2009 anymore.

There are people walking in huge groups
They have yellow stars on their coats
I turn around, not knowing where I am
And I see a lot of blown-up boats.

I finally recognise where I am
I'm in 1942
If you don't know what's happening
It's the middle of World War II.

Rebecca Morris (11)
Christie Park Primary School, Alexandria

Feelings

Sadness
Lonely, afraid,
Crying, thinking, weeping,
Blue-grey clouds, bright yellow sun,
Playing, smiling, laughing,
Cheerful, peaceful,
Happy.

Lauren Evans (11)

Christie Park Primary School, Alexandria

Animals

Whale
Slow, peaceful,
Eating, breathing, moving,
Spouting water, swept away,
Floating, swimming, living,
Small, bacteria,
Plankton.

Caitlyn Moore (11)
Christie Park Primary School, Alexandria

Hobbies

H opping along
O ver obstacles
B asketball
B aseball
I n the sports hall
E nergy failing
S wimming along.

Leigh Kennedy (10)
Christie Park Primary School, Alexandria

A Dragon

Fire breather
Scaly skin
Floating flyer
Mouldy mouth
Bad breath.

Jack McGauley (11)

Christie Park Primary School, Alexandria

Rumble Jungle

As I walk through the deadly jungle
I can hear a lot of animals
I can hear a rumble
And twigs snapping.

Tigers roaring and wild dogs
Monkeys swing from tree to tree
And down the path I can also hear the sea
I hear falling logs.

As I creep slowly
I can hear my friend Molly
Bugs and spiders crawl past me
And I can hear the waves crashing on the sea.

Blair Robertson (11)
Christie Park Primary School, Alexandria

World War II

W ar is a time when people get killed
O ars are what propel boats over the water
R ock foundations were used in the victorious war
L ogs were all over the forests at that time
D ads were home guards in the war

W ater was a problem when the war was on
A nti-aircraft guns were used to shoot planes
R age was in all Germans

T ugboats went up the Clyde then
W ar sirens went off most nights
O n the boats, men crossed their hearts.

Scott Brown (11)
Christie Park Primary School, Alexandria

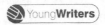
Space

S parkly stars fill the dark sky
P luto is the smallest
A stronauts enter space wearing heavy metal suits
C olourful planets surround the stars
E xciting place to be.

Natalie Hardie (10)

Christie Park Primary School, Alexandria

My Best Friend

M atthew is my best friend
Y ou would love to meet him

B elieve me, he's great
E xciting
S eriously funny
T errible dresser (joking)

F antastic goalkeeper
R eally cool
I sure did pick a good mate
E veryone likes him
N othing can make him sad
D on't get on his bad side though!

Gavin Thornton (11)
Christie Park Primary School, Alexandria

My Mum

Tea drinker
Biscuit biter
Quiet thinker
Rubbish fighter
Messy hair
My mum.

Sophie Clifford (11)
Christie Park Primary School, Alexandria

Sadness

S adness is when something bad happens
A ll you feel is lonely
D own and dull
N ever have I liked sadness
E nemy of joy
S adness makes you cry
S miles hate sadness, so soon go away.

Jack McFadyen (11)
Christie Park Primary School, Alexandria

The Beautiful Sea

Waves crashing against the rocks
Bits of water dripping from the docks
Splashing against the sand
The beautiful sea surrounds the land.

Under the water there's lots of darkness
They come out of dark holes and they're called fish
There are lots of dangers under the sea
That could easily eat you or me!

Jack Oliver (11)

Christie Park Primary School, Alexandria

My Dog

A mber is my pet dog
M y dog is quite crazy but very friendly
B acon is one of her favourite treats
E nergetic she is, but a good workout for me
R esting and running are her two hobbies.

Ross Manning (11)
Christie Park Primary School, Alexandria

Dragons

D angerous claws shred apart enemies
R aging fire shoots from the dragon's mouth
A gony comes to the unfortunate travellers
G ruesome deaths come to animals and humans
O utstanding flashes of light exit the cave
N oise and wailing come from the cave
S oaring to the sky with powerful wings.

Matthew McNeilly (11)

Christie Park Primary School, Alexandria

My Cousin

Cute, cuddly
Playful, joyful
Energetic, delightful
Mannerly, smiley
Happy, terror!

Heather McGlashan (11)
Christie Park Primary School, Alexandria

Fishing

F ishing is great fun
I nteresting fish
S tanding in the sun
H appy to catch a fish
I n the hut getting a cup of tea
N ylon in my fishing bag
G oing for a sleep while I wait.

Aaron McBride (11)

Christie Park Primary School, Alexandria

Limerick

There once was a hobbit named Dave
Who found a jewel in a cave
Then something went wrong
It was stolen by King Kong
Now he has a job as a slave.

Ross Alexzander Duncan (9)
Christie Park Primary School, Alexandria

The Dragon Limerick

There once was an old dragon
Who decided to live in a wagon
He could not breathe fire
'Cause he swallowed a wire
So he decided to go away in his wagon.

Lee McWhinney (10)

Christie Park Primary School, Alexandria

Deep Space Limerick

There once was a man in deep space
Who was about to tie his lace
He hit his head
He was not dead
But he had a mushed-up face.

Alistair Christopher Baird (10)
Christie Park Primary School, Alexandria

The Boy Named Jim

There once was a boy named Jim
And he didn't know how to swim
So he said to his mum,
'I fell on my bum.'
So he married his best friend Kim.

Chelsea Campbell (10)

Christie Park Primary School, Alexandria

Little Kitty Limerick

There once was a little kitty
Who lived in a big city
It tried to sing
When it fell in a bin
And everyone thought it was a pity.

Khaira Jayne McGlashan (10)
Christie Park Primary School, Alexandria

The Dog

There once was a dog called Daisy
She was always very lazy
She ate lots of food
And was always in a mood
Mrs Smart thought this was crazy!

Jennifer MacCalman (10)
Christie Park Primary School, Alexandria

Jungle

There once was a lion from Madagascar
Who wished he could run a little faster
He raced a cheetah
Who was a meat-eater
But it turned out a disaster.

Nicole Melville (10)

Christie Park Primary School, Alexandria

Polly's fling

As Polly danced the fling
She lost her engagement ring
It hit the ground
As she twirled around
As the audience had a dance and a sing.

Megan Buckley (10)
Christie Park Primary School, Alexandria

The Magic Box

(Based on 'Magic Box' by Kit Wright)

I will put in the box . . .
The first antler of a baby deer
The shiniest scale of a baby dragon
A shiny golden eagle.

I will put in the box . . .
The brightest star in the night sky
The whitest feather of an angel's wing
The biggest and brightest diamond.

My box is fashioned from clear ice, gold and silver spots
The hinges are made of shiny hard armour
The corners are made of love and friendship
I will take my box anywhere I go
And keep it on the loveliest planet in the galaxy.

Graeme Welsh (11)

David Livingstone Memorial Primary School, Blantyre

My Magic Box

(Based on 'Magic Box' by Kit Wright)

I will put in the box . . .
Some sparkling crystal
A handful of the finest stars in the whole planet
A lovely white horse with a shiny tail.

I will put in the box . . .
A breath of the finest water in history
A beautiful dragon flying forever
The first smile on a mother's face.

My box is fashioned from the finest gold in the world
And a strip of a lovely bit of blue ribbon
I will treasure my magic box forever
And I will take it everywhere with me.

Nicola Thomson (11)

David Livingstone Memorial Primary School, Blantyre

The Magic Box

(Based on 'Magic Box' by Kit Wright)

I will put in the box . . .
A football covered with golden fur from a lion
A strong elephant covered in Scottish flags
The lovely sand of the Sahara Desert.

I will put in the box . . .
The sound of a lovely little lamb baaing
The sound of two dragons fighting
A hot-air balloon with skinny little legs.

My box is fashioned from the skin of a wild tiger
Its hinges have the smooth touch of a cheetah
With its corners made from Rudolph's red nose.

I will play football with the box and take it everywhere
And keep it in a wonderful little cottage.

Dale Campbell (11)
David Livingstone Memorial Primary School, Blantyre

The Magic Box

(Based on 'Magic Box' by Kit Wright)

I will put in my magic box . . .
A beautiful ray of sun sweeping across the sky
A dog jumping and a family as happy as can be, together forever.

I will put in my magic box . . .
A flash of burning light
A fairy making a wish come true
And a fish learning how to swim.

My box is fashioned from a shining star
Fireworks and a lock from the antlers of a reindeer
Hand-carved from Turkey.

I shall roll down a hill and swim across the ocean with it
And let its spirits run *forever!*

Heather Neilson (11)

David Livingstone Memorial Primary School, Blantyre

All The Injuries

I once …
Broke my nose
Hurt my toes
Snapped my leg
Banged my head
Broke all my fingers
That really lingers
Hyper extended my wrist
Add that to the list
Punctured my spleen
Worst injury I've ever seen
Deadly frostbite
That's just not right
All the injuries made me scream
And I carried on till my face turned green!

Sean McAdam (11)
Deshar Primary School, Boat of Garten

Butterflies

B utterflies flutter by
U sing their wings to fly
T hey travel silently
T o find a flower
E ating nectar every hour
R eady to fly again
F lower to flower
L ovely butterflies flutter by
I n the sky
E very day I
S ee them in July.

Lucy Garrow (10)

Deshar Primary School, Boat of Garten

The Virgin Mk3

On the rails it goes *clitter-clatter*
At the speed of 100mph
With the wind going round it so fast
When it goes round the bend it's so loud
You can hear it go *whoosh*
Meanwhile, the passengers have their tea and biscuits
The ticket man sees your ticket
While the cook makes lovely food
The driver has the London to Glasgow service.

Jared Baker (10)
Deshar Primary School, Boat of Garten

Cheeky Monkeys

Cheeky monkeys
Climbing trees
Swinging from tree to tree
Munching on bananas
Eating goodies
Sometimes stealing local peelings
Cheeky monkeys
Way up high.

Carla Sermanni (11)

Deshar Primary School, Boat of Garten

The Beach – Haiku

Seaweed and lobster
Lying on the sandy beach
Rocks, pebbles, water.

Alex Young (8)
Kyle Primary School, Kyle of Loghalsh

Sea World – Haiku

Jellyfish swimming
Crabs nip badly when angry
Dolphins love to jump.

Siobhan McAllister (8)

Kyle Primary School, Kyle of Loghalsh

Space — Haiku

Stars, the moon, planets
They are all floating in space
That place is called space.

Caleb Wilson (7)

Kyle Primary School, Kyle of Loghalsh

Kraken Ride – Haiku

Watch the Kraken swim
In the sea and on the shore
Let's have a ride, yeah!

Hannah Butler (7)

Kyle Primary School, Kyle of Loghalsh

What Am I? – Haiku

I live in a field
You can get your milk from me
I am black and white.

Darren McBlain (10)
Netherthird Primary School, Cumnock

What Am I? – Haiku

I am white with fluff
I love eating lots of grass
I live in a field.

Shaun Alexander (10)
Netherthird Primary School, Cumnock

What Am I? — Haiku

I run very fast
I live in South Africa
I am gold and black.

Remy Grossmann (10)
Netherthird Primary School, Cumnock

What Am I? – Haiku

I have a long trunk
No animal can scare me
I make a racket!

Ryan McCallum (10)
Netherthird Primary School, Cumnock

What Am I? – Haiku

I like to eat grass
I'm related to a horse
I live in a herd.

Emma Lawson (10)
Netherthird Primary School, Cumnock

What Am I? – Haiku

I like to eat you
I like to eat some honey
I am black and white.

Abby Robinson (10)
Netherthird Primary School, Cumnock

What Am I? — Haiku

King of the jungle
Roaring out very loudly
I have a big mane.

Rebecca Walker (10)
Netherthird Primary School, Cumnock

What Am I? – Haiku

I have spiky teeth
I like to eat fish and snails
I live in water.

Louise Veitch (10)
Netherthird Primary School, Cumnock

What Am I? – Haiku

I like to eat you
I can be orange and black
I like to eat meat.

Calum Park (10)

Netherthird Primary School, Cumnock

What Am I? – Haiku

I am white with spots
Most people think I am cute
I have small black spots!

Amy Christie (10)
Netherthird Primary School, Cumnock

What Am I? — Haiku

I have floppy ears
I am afraid of foxes
I live in a hole.

Carly Wallace (10)
Netherthird Primary School, Cumnock

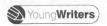

What Am I? – Haiku

I like to eat you
I am very vicious, yes
My best food is mice!

Charlotte Nolan (10)
Netherthird Primary School, Cumnock

What Am I? – Haiku

I live in a field
I love to run about lots
I love to eat grass.

Jade Reid (10)
Netherthird Primary School, Cumnock

What Am I? – Haiku

I live in a tree
I am from Australia
I hang from a tree.

Bobbie Young (10)
Netherthird Primary School, Cumnock

What Am I? – Haiku

I am a fatty
I have a big pair of ears
I have a long snout.

Kyle Alexander (9)
Netherthird Primary School, Cumnock

RRS Discovery

Ice-bashing
Cook-cooking
Scot-raging
Coal-falling
Ship-moving
Frostbitten-hands
Captain's-quarters
Iceberg-breaking
Stormy-clouds
Scary-ride.

Laura Mathieson (9)

Newfields Primary School, Dundee

The Discovery – Haiku

Robert Falcon Scott
The propeller is spinning
Dundee built the ship.

Amy Thomson
Newfields Primary School, Dundee

RRS Discovery — Haiku

The wind blows strongly
The snow falls high in the sky
Waves crash round the boat.

Emily Robertson
Newfields Primary School, Dundee

The Discovery

Thunder-crashing
Massive-boots
Dogs-barking
Cooks-cooking
Captain's-quarters
Ice-crashing
Wheel-spinning
Cold-weather
Bell-ringing
A scary ride indeed!

Sarah-Jane Hogan
Newfields Primary School, Dundee

The Discovery

Black-cat
Ashy-clouds
Crows-nest
Deck-washer
Captain-Scott
Heading-south
Shiny-helm
Working-propeller
Flaming-fire
Thunderous clouds.

Lee Hastie (8)

Newfields Primary School, Dundee

The Discovery

Bell-ringing
Boat-tipping
Boat-sailing
Cook-cooking
Men-eating
Ice-closing
Scott-raging
Yummy-seal
Awful-penguin
Ice-blowing.

Caitlyn Rose
Newfields Primary School, Dundee

The Discovery

Ice-blasting
Scott-raging
Scott's-cabin
Seals-yummy
Penguins-yucky
Big-boots
Boat-tipping
Men-sleeping
Men-writing
Hard-work.

Karis Penman (8)
Newfields Primary School, Dundee

RRS Discovery

D irty coal - dogs barking - dark rooms
I ce blasting - iceberg
S cott's cabin - ship sailing
C ooks cooking - cat chasing Captain Scott
O rdering food - overboard
V oyage - very cold - very wet
E xpedition - enormous seal
R ed rooms
Y oung man.

Katie Thorburn

Newfields Primary School, Dundee

Discovery

Captain Scott's-cabin
Ice-blasting
Very-wet
Icebergs-cold
Ship-sailing
Skeleton-cabin
Fire-burning
Ship-swaying
Snow-blowing
Ice-cracking.

Stephanie Barclay
Newfields Primary School, Dundee

Discovery

Ship-sailing
Engine-steaming
Wind-blowing
Ship-tipping
Ice-blasting
Scott's-cabin
Dishes-washing
Cooks-cooking
Crow's-nest.

Dean Kinmond (9)
Newfields Primary School, Dundee

RRS Discovery

Captain's-quarters
Waves-whooshing
Dirty-penguin
Angry-Scott
Propeller-spinning
Gangrene-bad
Dundee-boat
Dog-barking
Crow's-nest
Boat-moving.

Darcy Flanagan (9)
Newfields Primary School, Dundee

The Discovery

Ice-blasting
Thunder-clouds
Dogs-barking
Scott's-in charge
Bell-ringing
Scientists'-experiments
Awful-penguins
Boat-tipping
Crow's-nest
Man-falling.

Ryan Scobie
Newfields Primary School, Dundee

The Discovery

Ship in-Dundee
Scott-unhappy
Ship-stuck
Ice-breaks
Bad-weather
Scott-orders
Cold-ice
Thunder-clouds.

Jordan Cownie
Newfields Primary School, Dundee

Discovery Acrostic

D irty coal, dark clouds, dark room
I n ice, ice breaking
S cott's cabin, ship calling
C aptain Scott, cat chasing
O verboard, on the ice
V ery cold voyage
E xpedition, experiments
R inging bells, raised voices
Y ummy seal, yucky penguin.

Tia Steele
Newfields Primary School, Dundee

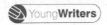

RRS Discovery

D ark room
I ce
S easick
C old sea
O riginal Discovery
V ery cold
E ating seal
R aging sea
Y ellow pillow.

Leon Reilly (8)
Newfields Primary School, Dundee

RRS Discovery

Ice-basher
Strong-ship
Supply-ship
Captain-Scott
Good-crew
Frozen-in
Propeller-spinning
Crow's-nest
Dirty-penguin
Bell-ringing
A cool ride.

William Dye
Newfields Primary School, Dundee

Discovery Acrostic

D undee
I ce breaker
S ea
C old and frosty
O n the ice
V isit the Discovery
E veryone frozen
R eally cold
Y oung men.

Thomas Dougal
Newfields Primary School, Dundee

The Discovery — Haiku

Robert Falcon Scott
Captain Scott is now in charge
Scott blew up the ice.

Jordan Martin
Newfields Primary School, Dundee

Winter Tree

Leaves blowing off the trees
The snow falling through the air
Branches curved in the snow
And then it starts all over again.

Josh Rendall (8)
Papdale Primary School, Kirkwall

Trees, Trees

Leaves, all types of colours,
Yellow, brown, red, gold,
Fall in autumn.
Green buds in spring,
Twigs cracking,
Seeds fly in the wild, strong winds,
Trees, fun to climb,
But watch out, you might fall.

Katy Diffin (8)
Papdale Primary School, Kirkwall

Winter Tree

Blowing branches,
Shaking while the wind goes through,
Rustle, rustle,
Bare branches,
Waiting for the snow,
What will come next?

Aimee Wells (7)
Papdale Primary School, Kirkwall

Trees

Bright green leaves on summery trees,
Budding buds in spring,
Trees are bare in winter,
Blossom trees are very nice,
Brown, thin branches,
Some trees get cut down
And are made into paper
And Christmas cards too,
Oh, I love trees,
Lovely trees.

Keri Heddle (7)

Papdale Primary School, Kirkwall

Winter Tree

Winter tree,
Thin and cold,
Trunk, trunk,
Brown as can be,
Branches, branches,
Long as can be,
Twigs, twigs,
Very, very pointy.

Glen Brough (7)
Papdale Primary School, Kirkwall

Trees, Trees

Trees, trees,
Covered in leaves,
Leaves, leaves,
Covered in ants,
Ants, ants,
Covered in dirt,
Then it starts again.

Graham Aim (8)
Papdale Primary School, Kirkwall

Winter Tree

Snowy, chilly,
Having fun,
Swinging, playing,
Having fun,
Looking forward
To spring,
Looking for buds.

Chloe Mulraine (7)

Papdale Primary School, Kirkwall

Fitness

Fit
That's it!
That's what I'm going to do,
It's true!
I'm going to play football, baseball,
Basketball too!

Fit,
That's it!
That's what I'm going to do,
It's true!
I'm going to do skateboarding, ping-pong,
Judo too!

Fit,
That's it!
That's what I'm going to do,
It's true!
I've achieved my goal,
Confident too!

Jake Kelly (8)
Ravenswood Primary School, Glasgow

Snow

Snow is cold, so wrap up warm
A winter storm, a winter storm
Now the storm's gone, we can go and play
Snow is falling this very day.

Snow is cold, so wrap up warm
A winter storm, a winter storm
Snow is white and very clear
Snow is very, very near.

Niamh Burrows (8)
Ravenswood Primary School, Glasgow

Snow

Snow is sparkling and so white
Open the window and smell the cold air
Wow! What can you see?
Little pawprints here and there
Wow! What can you feel?
White and fluffy snow
Wow! What can you hear?
Snowy birds chirping in white, shining trees.

Jennifer Gibson (9)
Ravenswood Primary School, Glasgow

Fun In The Snow

White, soft and very smooth
Snowy feet when you move
Snowballs flying everywhere
Snow also going in your hair.

The laughter of children having fun
The whole grey sky covering up the sun
When we go back in we can have some hot soup
But oh no, we will not have an ice cream scoop!

Adam Watson (8)

Ravenswood Primary School, Glasgow

Snowboarding

Snowboarding is fun,
Now the time's begun.
There I am up the hill,
I am full of chill
And I'm ready for the thrill!
I am sliding down,
Hearing that crackling of the snow
And as I feel the snow,
It goes up to freeze my nose!

Natalie McMeeking (8)
Ravenswood Primary School, Glasgow

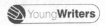

The Tiger

Meat eater
Loud roarer
Fire looker
Fast runner
Long tail
Super seeker
Great hunter
Sharp teeth
Orange black
My favourite!

David Triano (9)

St Cadoc's Primary School, Cambuslang

Dolphin

D iving champ
O lympic dolphin
L iving with his owner
P ull the rope
H ide before she comes
I n the sea she goes
N ot long till she is coming back.

Demi Lee Henderson (9)

St Cadoc's Primary School, Cambuslang

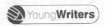

Giraffe

Long neck
Brown spots
Long legs
Big ears
Eats leaves
Small nose
Yellow skin
Spotty neck
Furry tail.

Collette Cavin (9)
St Cadoc's Primary School, Cambuslang

Monkey

Banana stealer
Tree swinger
Noise maker
Funny face
Furry animal
Long tail
Fast jumper
Nut cracker
Small face
Big family.

Casey Duffin (9)
St Cadoc's Primary School, Cambuslang

Crocodile

Ferocious teeth
Green scales
Scary predator
Amphibious animal
Tiger chaser
Young reptile
Man-eater
Water creature
Australian fighter.

Declan Reeves (9)

St Cadoc's Primary School, Cambuslang

Frogs And Tadpoles

Frogs,
Jumping, swimming,
Eating, diving, landing,
Catching flies, eating them,
Bursting out from frog spawn,
Wriggling, swimming, growing,
Eating, nibbling,
Tadpoles.

Holly McVey (9)
St Cadoc's Primary School, Cambuslang

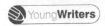

Swimming

High diver
Deep pool
Bouncing board
Armbands
Plastic goggles
Changing rooms
Numbered lockers
Wristband
Water floater
Swimming trunks.

Ross Thomson (9)
St Cadoc's Primary School, Cambuslang

Cheetah

Sporty cat
Yellow coat
Polka dot
Tree climber.

Solomon Rice (9)
St Cadoc's Primary School, Cambuslang

Stand Up To Hatred

Friend,
Comfortable, faithful,
Loving, comforting, enjoying,
Friends, relatives, bullies, countries,
Killing, terrifying, frightening,
Scary, hurtful,
Enemy.

Exclude,
Unwanted, bored,
Confusing, hurting, devastating,
Classmates, holocaust, friends, minorities,
Welcoming, laughing, sharing,
Supported, accepted,
Include.

Reiss Moran (9)

St Columbkille's Primary School, Glasgow

Stand Up To Hatred

Love,
Peaceful, happy,
Loving, caring, sharing,
Family, friends, bullies, borders,
Terrifying, hurting, killing,
Unfair, sad,
Hate.

War,
Wrong, dreadful,
Killing, abusing, shocking,
Weapons, armies, prayers, God,
Living, singing, reading,
Joyful, happy,
Peace.

Lauren O'Reilly (9)
St Columbkille's Primary School, Glasgow

Stand Up To Hatred

Love,
Beautiful, strong,
Loving, caring, sharing,
Pets, parents, relatives, friends,
Bullying, hurting, fighting,
Unfair, horrific,
Hate.

War,
Wrong, dreadful,
Horrifying, shocking, terrifying,
Armies, battlefields, weapons, soldiers,
Calming, sleeping, resting,
Joyful, happy,
Peace.

Mhairi Cowden (9)
St Columbkille's Primary School, Glasgow

Stand Up To Hatred

Love,
Happy, peaceful,
Caring, sharing, loving,
Parents, God, relatives, friends,
Hurting, terrifying, killing,
Unfair, sad,
Hate.

War,
Dreadful, loathful,
Shocking, abusing, upsetting,
Bullies, countries, borders, nationalities,
Forgiving, reading, partying,
Joyful, happy,
Peace.

Alan Paulson (8)

St Columbkille's Primary School, Glasgow

Stand Up To Hatred

Hate,
Horrific, angry,
Frightening, destructive, excluding,
Bullies, countries, borders, nationality,
Heart-warming, caring, loving,
Peaceful, happy,
Love.

Exclude,
Afraid, shy,
Upsetting, shocking, boring,
Strangers, friends, classmates, bullies,
Sharing, playing, talking,
Cheery, safe,
Include.

Heather Bowles (9)

St Columbkille's Primary School, Glasgow

Stand Up To Hatred

War,
Tough, dreadful,
Killing, abusing, upsetting,
Weapons, soldiers, candles, prayers,
Sleeping, living, reading,
Happy, joyful,
Peace.

Love,
Peaceful, happy,
Caring, loving, helping,
Family, friends, bullies, nationality,
Heart-breaking, killing, frightening,
Unfair, angry,
Hate.

Megan Neilly (9)
St Columbkille's Primary School, Glasgow

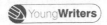

Lord Of The Rings

L ord and kings fight for glory
O ut battling for peace
R aging Gollum's after the one Ring
D warf Gimli is brave, that's why he fights

O verall, Orcs have more people
F ighting for peace and destruction is everywhere

T ime for war has come
H atred between Orcs and men of the west
E very day people die for hope of men

R ampaging into the White City
I ndestructible Ring got thrown into the ferocious fire
N ever will Orcs trouble men and the Shire again
G lory comes to Middle Earth and to Frodo Baggins
S hire is in peace thanks to men, elves and dwarves.

Michael Haughey (8)
St Columbkille's Primary School, Glasgow

The Sea

T remendous waves go up and down
H eavy oceans crash the rocks
E ach and every one of them

S ees the sun go down
E veryone watches in silence
A nd by the sea, sits me.

Serena Piacentini (8)
St Columbkille's Primary School, Glasgow

Kennings Poem

Tail-chaser
Fast-runner
Quick-eater
Loud-barker
Food-lover
Adult-hater
Far-jumper
Stick-chewer
Face-licker
A good-friend for me.

Shannon Graham (8)
St Columbkille's Primary School, Glasgow

The Jungle

T he jungle is my life
H ere there are animals
E nemies in the jungle hunting for animals

J ungle so green, so beautiful
U sually it's hot and steamy all over the place
N ight-time is cool and peaceful
G ood animals and bad animals
L ots of trees in the breeze
E very animal is happy in the jungle.

Amy Dunsmuir (8)
St Columbkille's Primary School, Glasgow

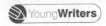

The Sea

As I dived into the shiny, blue sea,
I started swimming,
I saw a lot of clownfish.
Then I couldn't believe my eyes!
I saw a dolphin!
But it was too late - my gas tank was empty
And I didn't get to see any of the other creatures.

Niamh Lafferty (8)
St Columbkille's Primary School, Glasgow

Kennings

Ball-chaser
Cat-hater
Door-scratcher
Long-walker
Tail-biter
Toe-licker
Loud-barker
Stick-chewer
Fast-runner
Owner-liker.

Lauren Angus (9)
St Columbkille's Primary School, Glasgow

The Sea

See the boat sailing on the sparkling sea,
I'm eating fish and chips,
At the deep blue water's edge, I built a big sandcastle,
Now the wicked water is washing it away.

Chloe Stirrat (7)

St Columbkille's Primary School, Glasgow

The Sea

T he holidays are here!
H anging out with my family
E ating an ice cream cone

S wimming in the sea with dolphins
E ating fish and chips
A t the seaside building a sandcastle.

Cara Dearie (8)
St Columbkille's Primary School, Glasgow

Kennings Poem

Tail-splasher
Hair-brusher
Sea-hider
Starfish-lover
Wave-swimmer
Splendid-singer
Prince-lover
Happy-princess
Mirror-looker
Dolphin-lover.

Saskia Foy (8)
St Columbkille's Primary School, Glasgow

Dolphins

D elighted dolphins jumping out the sea
O ther people love them
L oving them and caring for them
P eople giving them fish
H aving fun swimming with them
I watch everything that they do with them
N ow I want to swim with them too.

Christiana Kelly (8)
St Columbkille's Primary School, Glasgow

Kennings Poem

Vine-swinger
Tree-climber
Banana-eater
Food-stealer
Playful-pretender
Creative-creature
Human-like
Intelligent-animal
Long-jumper
Coconut-cracker.

Aaron Clark (8)
St Columbkille's Primary School, Glasgow

Kennings Poem

Tail-chaser
Fast-eater
Cat-hater
Stick-chewer
Ball-lover
Ankle-biter
Loud-barker
High-jumper
A good friend for me.

Broghan Grant (8)
St Columbkille's Primary School, Glasgow

Video Games

V ery good at Fifa '09
I always beat my dad at it
D ifferent from Fifa '08
E very single match I win, I get a trophy
O nly children know the football tricks

G ames are the best
A brilliant goal by me
M um says, 'Get that off!'
E ven if I play it in my bedroom
S ince then my mum has said I can't play it until Monday!

Kyle McCole (8)
St Columbkille's Primary School, Glasgow

Winter

W atching snowflakes settle silently
I just love watching the snowflakes fall
N ot long till Christmas comes
T he reindeer having a hard time
E lves busy making toys all night
R eindeer helping Santa with the presents.

Fergus Edwards (8)
St Columbkille's Primary School, Glasgow

Kennings Poem

Cat-chaser
Fussy-eater
Toy-player
Tail-wagger
Good-sniffer
Bath-hater
Finger-biter
Shoe-chewer
Wall-scratcher
Owner-lover.

Anna Carr (8)

St Columbkille's Primary School, Glasgow

Kittens

K ittens watch their owner's eyes
I love the way they jump and play
T aking them to the vet when they're ill
T hanking them for all their fun
E ating, eating lots and lots
N ever ignoring people's attention
S mall kittens fit in your hands.

Maria Lalley (8)
St Columbkille's Primary School, Glasgow

Mythical Creatures

Long, long ago, in a land in the sky,
All the dragons began to cry.
'What is happening?' asked the leader.
Nobody answered for they'd all turned to stone.

Long, long ago, in a land underwater,
All the mermaids began to cry.
'What is happening?' asked the king.
Nobody answered for they'd all turned to stone.

Long, long ago, in a place near a castle,
All the unicorns began to cry.
'What is happening?' asked the queen.
Nobody answered for Medusa had returned!

Eve McIntosh (10)
St Joseph's Primary School, Bonnybridge

Vampires

They hide in the dark,
They fly in the night,
There's nothing there to see,
Nobody in sight,
Until … they bite you that night!

From dusk to dawn,
They reign in the sky,
Until sunlight comes
They hide in disguise.
But then, when moonlight comes again,
They bite and bite and bite again.

Daniel Walshe (10)
St Joseph's Primary School, Bonnybridge

Basketball

B asketball is really great
A very great jump shot
S ee all the tall players
K entucky is my favourite team
E at all the hot dogs
T eam talk at half-time
B ig tall man takes a free throw
A fter half-time they get back to the game
L ove the game
L ove basketball.

Lewis Bell (11)
St Joseph's Primary School, Bonnybridge

The Jungle

The snakes hide in the bushes,
And the panthers hide in the trees.
The gorilla just walks around
And sits on its knees.

The monkeys swing from vines
And the bears eat honey.
The lizards make chimes
And that's really funny.

Parrots fly high in the air,
The leopard grooms its hair.
The cheetah plays poker
And thinks he's the Joker.

And that's the jungle,
Be careful not to fumble.

Tyler Sams (11)
St Joseph's Primary School, Bonnybridge

Climate Change

Climate change is such a bad thing,
The world will change into a big, watery spring.
But if we change our ways right now,
We may save the world and animals, but how?
I know the world is feeling sad,
So let's work together till we go mad.
When we are finished, we can all say,
I can't believe we saved the world in two thousand and nine!

Connor Hazlett (9)
St Joseph's Primary School, Bonnybridge

What Am I?

I am small
I love to swim
I come in all sorts of colours
I don't make a sound
I have a small tail
Oh, and I have bubbles coming out of my mouth.

What am I?

Kelsey Differ (11)
St Lucy's Primary School, Abronhill

What Am I?

I live in the sea
I am blue or grey
And very smart
And love fish

What am I?

Darren Elliott (11)

St Lucy's Primary School, Abronhill

Who Am I?

Some people annoy me
Some people adore me
I fetch for sticks
I have fleas and ticks
I chase my tail
And bring in the mail.

Who am I?

Megan Kennedy (11)
St Lucy's Primary School, Abronhill

Scotland

S ome amazing sights
C onstant mince and tatties
O h flower of Scotland.
T artan kilts
L ots of haggis
A lot of football
N o place like it.
D ead proud to be living in Scotland.

Alistair Russell (11)
St Lucy's Primary School, Abronhill

My Dog, Rascal

Scruffy mutt,
Red collar,
Pampered pooch,
Tail wagger,
Active pup,
Happy puppy,
Sharp teeth,
Long claws,
Sensitive whiskers,
Black fur,
Cute cuddler,
Always hungry,
Fast runner.

Caitriona Houston (11)
St Lucy's Primary School, Abronhill

My School

The sky is blue with dots of white.
The sun is always shining bright.
We're sitting inside working hard,
And soon we'll be playing out in the yard.
Everyone in the school has a special job to do,
But someone will still lose an indoor shoe!
Our school is the best, no doubt about that
And our janitor, Mr Martin, will chase away any old rat.
I'm in Primary 7 and I'll be in high school soon.
I've heard it's just as exciting as going to the moon!
Now I must say goodbye,
I've some work to do.
I'm going onto maths now,
So I'll see you soon.

Rachel McKinlay (11)
St Lucy's Primary School, Abronhill

My 1 Litre Water Bottle

I have a 1 litre water bottle that is black,
It has eyes, a nose and a hairy back.
He has a mouth too but it is never opened,
His name is Admiral but nobody knows,
It has two hand grips at the sides for me to use;
At night he's still and quiet,
At morning he's up and active,
But when he runs out of water,
He's weak and needs a refill,
And when he gets a refill,
He's up and active again.

Ross Kavanagh (11)
St Lucy's Primary School, Abronhill

What Am I?

I fly in the sky
I have beautiful wings
My colour is very bright
You might see me at a lake
What am I?

I'm a dragonfly.

Martine Baird (11)
St Lucy's Primary School, Abronhill

When I Dream ...

I sit by my window
Quiet as can be
Fall asleep
Mind finally free.

I see a picture
What can it be?
A far away land
Across the sea.

It has ...
Pure blue grass
Clear green sky
Birds on the ground
And mice which fly.

Paths that lead far away
Twist and turn
Amongst the grey
And white trees.

The image fades
Eyes flicker awake
Into reality
Out of fake.

Alanah Collins (11)
St Michael's Primary School, Port Glasgow

Statues

Statues sit and stare at you
With beady little eyes.
They're such scary things to see
When you're alone.

They're very creepy
Like china dolls
On a shelf.

They sit silently
On a wall
Or window sill
Not moving a muscle.

But people say
Whenever you turn away
They creep up closer on you
And go *'Boo!'*

Kyle McKay (11)
St Michael's Primary School, Port Glasgow

What I Saw

I saw a snail
Quite pale,
Picked it up
By the tail.
It died.

I saw a bee
Followed me,
Ran like a fool
Up nearest tree.
I fell.

I saw a cow
It took a bow,
Thought it would
Be up by now.
Still there.

Debbie McGowan (11)
St Michael's Primary School, Port Glasgow

Seven Stars

When the sun is out
The Great Bear hides in fear
Sheltering somewhere dark
Till the moon defends her territory.
Finally The Plough shows itself
Smiling down on all who care to look,
Casting its silver gaze around the landscape
From the soft velvet sky around it.
The Big Dipper looks down
At the whispering willow
The staring sycamore
And the breathtaking beech.
When the trees see this magnificent constellation
Scooping up the sky
They smile and whisper goodnight
Before yawning . . .
Drifting . . .
Sleeping . . .

Emma Scott (11)
St Michael's Primary School, Port Glasgow

Walking Home

I'm walking home, it's very dark.
I suddenly hear a dog bark
In the shadows.

The shop lights are out
They're closed, without a doubt
. . . I'm late.

I hear footsteps coming from behind
I look around wondering what I'll find
I see nothing.

Alana Power (11)

St Michael's Primary School, Port Glasgow

My Great Gran Is A Super Gran

My great gran, 92 years old
She's still fit and healthy
Even goes to the bingo!

She is a very good dancer
Up at parties shimmering away
Then falling asleep with crisps in her hands

Turning on the TV as she wakes up
Still half sleeping, flicking through the channels
Eyes wide open as she hears EastEnders' tune

She has children of her own
Grandchildren, great grandchildren and even
Great, great grandchildren
But I love my great gran more than all!

Demi Scott (11)
St Michael's Primary School, Port Glasgow

My Clarinet

Shiny black
Sometimes loud
Sometimes quiet
Never shy
Put together
One piece
By one
High notes
Low notes
Joyful tunes
Sad tunes
Squeaks, *ouch!*
My favourite clarinet.

Nicole Ali (11)
St Michael's Primary School, Port Glasgow

Sorted

I'm glad that it has stopped,
The bullying that was happening.
I didn't like it at all,
Being punched and them laughing at me.

The bullies' names were ordinary
Just like Bob and Tami,
It wasn't the names that hurt me
But what they would do.

I was in the cloakroom
Hanging my coat on my hanger,
They pulled me from behind,
I couldn't see anything,
Smelly fingers all over my face.

The last straw,
Finally I decided I had had enough.
Went to the head teacher's office,
Knocked on the door and went in,
Told it all.
Sorted!

Joanne McAulay (11)
St Michael's Primary School, Port Glasgow

Music Is My Life

M usical notes, crotchets and quavers
U nusual effects, from lighters or scissors
S ongs and melodies, with different styles of tuning
I like to play different types like rock or jazz or blues
C reate my own original version of 'The Godfather' theme,
 like Slash did.

Nathan Middleton (11)
St Michael's Primary School, Port Glasgow

My Computer

I'm positive there's a tiny being, living inside my computer,
His hair is as blue as the sea and his face is as bright as the night.
He wears a silver galactic T-shirt and dark denim jeans.

He only has one friend - the mouse,
Who lies all day on the mat.
The mouse just sits and waits until someone wants to surf the Net,
He does it too, but he hasn't learned much yet.

I wonder how this tiny being finds his way around,
With all the websites, folders and piles of files,
Saving this and saving that,
Deleting things here and there,
The recycle bin doesn't care.

It must be very lonely,
To be the only being in software,
With no family or many friends but I suppose you get used to it.
I think for it, it's an everyday thing,
Surfing the Net, for an online vet in case mouse gets sick!

Olivia Gillen (11)
St Michael's Primary School, Port Glasgow

My Little Brother

My little brother
Can be a menace
Running through my room

My little brother
Can be annoying
Wanting to play all the time

My little brother
Can be funny
When doing his hyper dance

My little brother
Can be cute
Giving me puppy-dog eyes

But my little brother
Is my best friend
Now and always will be

Erin Montgomery (11)
St Michael's Primary School, Port Glasgow

Eye Opener

I am blind
I cannot see
I forgot to bring
My glasses with me.

What was that?
I'm quite scared,
I don't know
What I just heard.

I need the toilet,
I cannot see,
Where's the loo roll?
I require it urgently.

Then I walk out,
I open my eyes ...

That would explain a lot!

Rachel McColgan (11)
St Michael's Primary School, Port Glasgow

Leaves In The Autumn

I wake up in the morning
I know that autumn is near
Although it's cold and icy
I know there's nothing to fear

Leaves gently fall around me
Looking so happy and free
But the trees look sad and lonely
Over the loss of their leaves

Autumn time is so wonderful
Although the weather's not great
All the children love playing
Although we can't stay out too late

Laura Pettigrew (11)
St Michael's Primary School, Port Glasgow

Under My Bed

Under my bed is a long-lost world
I've never dared to look
I think I'm going to have a peek
My stomach really hurts now
I head for the door ready to go
Stop myself and say
'No, I have got to do this once and for all!'

Start to go under
Feel a little scared
Go right back to wall
Feel something hit my leg
'Argh!' I say as something hits my leg
To my relief it's only my socks!
'Phew!' I get out from under my bed
And feel scared no more.

Nicola McGowan (11)

St Michael's Primary School, Port Glasgow

Snowflake

The time has come to join you all
I float down from the sky
I lay a blanket of snow on the ground
I can hear the sound of birds chirping and singing
But I am starting to get scared
Because all the snow is going away
But hopefully I will come back another day.

Georgina Glancy (11)
St Michael's Primary School, Port Glasgow

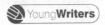

Escaping From The Cops

I quickly run without a pause
Trying to think what did I cause?
Maybe it was shop-lifting, no that's not true,
Or it could have just been me hanging with the crew.

I turn around to see if they are there,
Oh no, they are, but I don't care.
I've been running for a while,
Maybe for a mile.

Suddenly they catch me,
I think I'll just go silently.
They handcuff me and then put me in the car
And then I remember.

It was in the bar!

Gina Meahan (11)
St Michael's Primary School, Port Glasgow

Leaves Are Falling With A Breeze

All the trees are unloading their leaves
The fear of losing toes is looming
Among the maple trees.
With all the departed leaves
All ready for the frosty days ahead.

The crunchy sound is everywhere
Rustling like the wind
All the beautiful and colourful leaves
Are falling with a breeze.

Sean McGerr (11)
St Michael's Primary School, Port Glasgow

Maths Poem

M aths fills my brain with lots of knowledge.
A jotter, a workbook and a textbook lying in front of me.
T he teacher's explaining but I know what to do.
H arder every time I try to get it all done in time.
S hout hip hip hooray, as I got it all done today.

Melissa Macreath (11)

St Michael's Primary School, Port Glasgow

Robert Burns

Robert Burns is a famous Scot from Ayrshire
He had a keen ear for music
Sometimes he wrote poems to suit old Scottish tunes

He wrote the lowland Scottish language
And he wrote speeches for English lessons at school
Robert Burns is our national Bard
Some poems are in foreign languages
But also translated into Scottish

2009 is the 250th birthday of Robert Burns
Happy Birthday, Rabbie.

Graeme Stevenson (11)
St Michael's Primary School, Port Glasgow

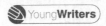

Eiffel Tower

E verybody knows
I nto Paris I go
F lying in the air
F lying so slow
E verybody eats
L anding on the ground

T here it was, what a sight
O n the top, what a big spike
W herever I go
E veryone sees
R emember it please.

Sam Mallen (9)
Stenton Primary School, Stenton

Tyranitar

T he beast looks like a bull
Y ou could not imagine it in your wildest dreams
R are creature, it is
A nd it is very dangerous
N o one would go near it
I t carries an axe on its back
T here are 56 left in the world
A mystical creature it is
R eally you should watch out!

Alex Cummings (8)
Stenton Primary School, Stenton

Cheeky Cat

Once there was a greedy cat,
He ate anything but bacon fat.
He would eat apple peel and paper bags,
He would even eat old cleaning rags.
He used to have a dog food bowl,
And it had a picture of a baby mole.
If you left some soup with no lid
Then you'd wish you never did,
If you found him eating the soup
The next thing you'd know he'd be running into the chicken coop.

Lucy Allan (8)
Stenton Primary School, Stenton

Scotland

S cotland is a good place to live.
C rops grow there in the field.
O ver the hills and down the valleys.
T ill the day is dawn.
L iving in Scotland is cool.
A ll the people work hard.
N ever disobey living in Scotland
D o have fun living in Scotland.

Ewan Brown (9)

Stenton Primary School, Stenton

The Dog

I have a dog, his name is Bob
And he is a big slob. Sometimes he is a cutie.
My dad says he is a wee beauty.
I like to take him on a really long walk.
When he looks at me sometimes
I wish he would talk.
He eats a lot of bones when he roams.
Even although he is a big slob,
He is still my dog Bob.

Brodie Beveridge (8)
Stenton Primary School, Stenton

White Rhinoceros

White rhinoceros I hate, I hate
How they jump and swing
I just really hate.
They really have a big, big brain
Even when they fall asleep

Rhinoceros' go in the water
Have great big horns and tough big eyes.
In the zoo I see them
Now although I know they are
Oh I wish they were not there at all
Continuously thinking they know the best
Even when they are doing anything.
So often they do silly things
Sometimes in the *mud!*

Mhairi MacDonald (9)
Stenton Primary School, Stenton

My Magic Unicorn

M y magic unicorn flies high in the sky
Y ou may see her, I don't know why.

M y unicorn's name is Stella
A nd her best friend's name is Bella.
G o down to the river
I f you want to see her,
C ome with me and try not to feed her

U sually when you go she will jump out at you.
N ow go wild.
I get a ride on her back,
C ome on then go home
O r she will attack.
R un along home tonight,
N ow is the time before you get a fright!

Olivia Gillespie (11)
Stenton Primary School, Stenton

Brothers

B rothers these days,
R unning around in the house
O ut of control.
T hinking they know best.
H iding your best toys.
E ating with their mouths open.
R eally getting on my nerves.
'S o what!' I hear them say, 'you love us anyway!'

India Sinclair (9)
Stenton Primary School, Stenton

Teachers

T eachers, they teach us all day at school.
E nd of term trips they plan for us.
A nd they give us loads of homework to do.
C hecking homework that we bring.
H elping us when we need help.
E very teacher is different in a way.
R eally good at doing maths.
S chool and teachers are made for each other.

Natalie Smith (10)

Stenton Primary School, Stenton

Friends

F riends are what you want in school,
R eally great ones,
I wouldn't want to live without.
E ach person should have that one special friend.
N ew friends can be great,
D epending on the traits they've got.
S o be sure to tell your best friend how great they really are!

Izzy Wilson-Beales (10)
Stenton Primary School, Stenton

Running and Walking

Walking through my favourite shop,
Walking through my favourite wood,
Walking through my favourite town,
Walking through my favourite door,
Walking through my favourite country,
Walking through my favourite house,
Oh! What a lot of walking, I think I will start running.

Running through a field of straw,
Running through an icy river,
Running through a park of children,
Running through a valley of butterflies,
Running through small shallow puddles,
Running through a jungle so small,
Oh! I feel tired with all this running,
I think I will sit down.

Katrina Maguire (9)
Stenton Primary School, Stenton

America

America the beautiful, is the place I would like to be,
Out of civilisation,
Up so high in the Flatiron mountains,
That's the place for me.

Mountain lions stalking, looking for their prey,
Bears hunting elk
With fur of shining silk,
That's the place for me.

Yellow dried up grasses swaying in the breeze,
Red leaves, orange leaves,
Falling from the trees,
That's the place for me.

Big red sheets of rock cover the mountains high,
Massive boulders cover the land,
And vast amounts of plain,
That's the place for me.

America the beautiful, is the place I would like to be,
I would love to see the shining sun,
Floating in the blue sky.
America, that has to be the place for me.

Arthur Sinclair (11)
Stenton Primary School, Stenton

Football

Every day I look in
The mirror and say
To myself I wish
I could be a footballer.

I wish, I wish I could
Have the style of Beckham,
The skill of Ronaldo, and
Dribble as fast as the money
That will be running through
My hands.

I wish, I wish every time
I enter the field there
Would be banners saying
Wing Wizard Salkeld.

I wish, I wish I could
Be the captain of my of home country,
Scotland of course,
And win the World Cup five times in a row.

As I blow out the candles on
My cake, I wish, I wish I
Could be a footballer.

Thomas Salkeld (11)
Stenton Primary School, Stenton

Animal Kingdom

Animals big and small
Noisy and loud, short and tall
Imaginative, colourful
Mammals, reptiles
All over, even in the Isles
Lions, elephants, tigers too
My quest to find a new animal

Kangaroos, koalas, wallabies too
Into the Oz world I go
Imaginative, colourful
Lazy, lying koalas
Jumping, energetic kangaroos
Wandering, lonely wallabies
My quest to find a new animal

Monkeys, lemurs, gorillas too
Into the rainforest I go
Imaginative, colourful
Grizzly, grumpy gorillas
Menacing, magic monkeys
Luscious, large lemurs
My quest to find a new animal

Dolphins, whales, seals too
Into the ocean I go
Imaginative, colourful
Dopey, dancing dolphins
Whopping great big whales
Slippy, slimy seals
My quest to find a new animal

Into a newfound habitat I go
I rest my weary head
I will continue my quest tomorrow
For now I need my bed.

Ailsa Maguire (11)
Stenton Primary School, Stenton

Stenton Primary School

S tenton Primary is a lovely place
T o learn things.
E verybody is kind and helpful.
N obody is mean.
T he teachers explain things very clearly.
O ne big family we are at Stenton.
N obody is single at Stenton School.

P oems we love to write.
R eady to get our pencils on the paper.
I n the classroom we help people who are stuck.
M eeting new people makes everyone happy.
A t Stenton we can be smart.
R eady in the morning to go to school.
Y eah we love Stenton School.

S tenton is
C overed with brilliant students.
H appy everyone is.
O h how Stenton School is, learning all the time.
O h happy the children are.
L aughing all the time.

Megan Smith (9)
Stenton Primary School, Stenton

Home Haikus

I wish to go home
To the country that I love
I dream of my home

Different people
Often ask me why I came
To live in this place

Warm in the summer
But snow in the winter yeah
I really love it

There's Blackpool Tower
And there's Big Ben in London
And then our Queen too

Can you guess the place?
My special, special country
England is my home

Caroline Logan (11)
Stenton Primary School, Stenton

My Family

F amilies are cool, together by the pool
A nd I love my family, playing games merrily
M y mum is so funny, and looks after the money
I think my sisters are vain and a very big pain
L ike my dad, I have brown eyes; he gives us cuddles
when each of us cries
Y et together they are the best family I've got!

Katie Stuart (8)
Stenton Primary School, Stenton

St Bernards

S wiss national dog (and I can see why)
T he hero of the mountain

B rilliant in the snow
E ager to save the people
R acing to save the skiers and boarders carrying brandy
   in his barrel
N othing can stop me from loving them
A nd it's because they're cute and are ever so friendly
R eally, really big, with a big heart to match
D ogs are up for a competition when this big hero arrives
S t Bernards are the best, and if they don't win your heart they
   definitely win mine!

Alexandra Stuart (11)
Stenton Primary School, Stenton

Impossible Dreams

In my dreams I travel to the future and the past.
I fight evil from the future and the past.
If you come with me you'll be ... in danger.
I see Daleks and Cybermen and aliens too
So don't come with me or you will get sucked into a different world,
A world where I will never see you again.
A world that is in the sun and you will die.

Oliver Aitchison (8)
Strathblane Primary School, Glasgow

Mrs Simpson

Mrs Simpson is fun but strict.
Mrs Simpson believes she is young.
Mrs Simpson is artistic and kind.
Mrs Simpson is funny.
Mrs Simpson doesn't like leaning over you to mark your work.
Mrs Simpson is frightening when she gets angry.
But in the end you can't get any better.

Jamie Macfarlane (10)
Taynuilt Primary School, Taynuilt

The Girls In My Class

All the girls in my class, including me,
Are all so witty,
Thinking that we're so pretty.
We fight and we moan with others,
Then the boys come over like our funny little brothers.
We get in trouble when we fiddle with our hair,
But by the end of it we look like a bear.

Us girls in the class, we're not that bad,
But if you say something horrible we will get sad.
When we get changed for PE we stay there forever,
Chatting away and looking in the mirror.
You can't blame us, we're not going crazy,
We just have some moments when we get very lazy.
Us girls in the class, we are a nice bunch,
But we get pretty greedy when it comes to lunch!

Maeve Hannigan (11)
Taynuilt Primary School, Taynuilt

Curry

Curry is tasty,
Curry is hot,
Curry is brilliant,
I like it a lot.
Curry in the morning,
Curry for tea,
Curry is amazing,
When it's just for me.
Curry is spice,
It tastes so nice,
I love it with rice.
Curry with chips,
Curry nips,
I don't know what could be better.

Amy Boyce (11)
Taynuilt Primary School, Taynuilt

Silent Reading

(For Ruby, John, William, Georgia and Bump)

Everyone is quiet,
Heads are down,
Slowly the heads rise,
As the teacher exits the room.
Yes!
Susie starts it off,
By throwing a piece of Blue-Tac at Peter!
Peter has now turned around,
He's picking up the Blue-Tac and ...
Oh no! He has missed.
Jessica thinks he threw it at her,
And now she's rolling up her sleeves.
She has taken a swing,
But has hit Mary!
Now it is turning into a cat fight.
The boys are laughing . . .
Wait, someone is coming,
It's the *teacher!*
Everyone has frozen,
They're all in trouble,
I'm just lucky no one will get me into trouble;
Because no one blames the
Assistant teacher!

Caitlin Taylor (11)
Taynuilt Primary School, Taynuilt

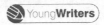

My Home

My home is in the village called Taynuilt,
Next to rows and rows of houses.
My home is a home where I can rest,
Or do fun things to my heart's content.
My home smells of garden plants,
Picked freshly from patches and put in jars.
My home has a long backyard,
Used by the chickens and shared with the plants.
My home is my dream place,
For a child like me.

Sam Lines (11)

Taynuilt Primary School, Taynuilt

The Fire

The fire is bright.
The fire is warm.
The fire is dangerous.
The fire is calm.
The fire is dancing.
The fire is light.
I wish the fire was alight.
Please Mum, light the fire.

Daniel Day (11)
Taynuilt Primary School, Taynuilt

Home To Me

I am football crazy because it keeps me fit.
Football means the world to me,
What would I do without it?
I'm a pretty good player,
But I don't like to boast.
But football is my favourite thing,
And I will always love it the most.

David Orr (11)
Taynuilt Primary School, Taynuilt

My Home To Me

My home to me is welcoming.
My home to me is nice and warm.
My home to me is full of cuddles.
My home to me is a night-time's sleep.
My home to me is a bird's midnight song.
My home to me is like visiting the moon.
My home to me is a five star hotel.
My home to me is just mine.

Anja Powell (10)
Taynuilt Primary School, Taynuilt

My Home

In my home, I have lots of settees and chairs,
But that's not what I feel is special about my home.

I have plenty of space in my house and a big garden
to run around in,
But that's not what I feel is special about my home.

My home smells of baking,
But that's not what I feel is special about my home.

In my home I have my family,
That's what I feel is special about my home.

Cailean Wilkinson (10)
Taynuilt Primary School, Taynuilt

My Family

My father he is flammable,
It says so on his coat.
My mother she's going cannibal,
She just ate my pet goat!
My sister sells conkers,
She's saving for a mouse,
I'm going bonkers living in this house!

Carol Armstrong (11)
Torthorwald Primary School, Torthorwald

Sunday Bake

It's a Sunday and I thought I would bake,
But oh what to make?
I'll get some milk that is deliciously cool
And white as snow,
Now that's in the bowl and ready to mix,
So here we go, *whip, whip, whip!*

Now it doesn't look just right so I'll get
Some raisins all large and brown,
Now the eggs with yolks golden-yellow as the sun,
I hope when I put it in the oven it doesn't burn,
So here we go, *whip, whip, whip!*

No, still not right, perhaps it needs more mix,
Let's try some castor sugar that runs through my fingers like sand.
Now for the finishing touch, some brandy, butter and flour.
Whoops, too much, now it looks like glue!

Patricia McKerlie
Torthorwald Primary School, Torthorwald

Young Writers Information

We hope you have enjoyed reading this book - and that you will continue to enjoy it in the coming years.

If you like reading and writing poetry drop us a line, or give us a call, and we'll send you a free information pack.

Alternatively if you would like to order further copies of this book or any of our other titles, then please give us a call or log onto our website at www.youngwriters.co.uk

Young Writers Information
Remus House
Coltsfoot Drive
Peterborough
PE2 9JX
(01733) 890066